Earth's Environment
in Danger

# Natural Resource Depletion

Micah Sanchez

**PowerKiDS** press

New York

Published in 2018 by The Rosen Publishing Group, Inc.
29 East 21st Street, New York, NY 10010

First Edition

Editor: Elizabeth Krajnik
Book Design: Rachel Rising

Photo Credits: Cover iStockphoto.com/hsvrs; Cover, pp. 1, 3, 4, 6, 8, 10, 12, 14, 16, 18, 19, 20, 21, 22, 23, 24 ALKRO/Shutterstock.com; p. 4 Aphelleon/ Shutterstock.com; p. 5 vvoe/Shutterstock.com; p. 7 bondgrunge/Shutterstock.com; p. 8 WDG Photo/Shutterstock.com; p. 9 James Jones Jr/Shutterstock.com; p. 11 Rudmer Zwerver/Shutterstock.com; p. 13 Auscape/Universal Images Group/ Getty Images; p. 15 Konstantnin/Shutterstock.com; p. 16 Kametaro/Shutterstock.com; p. 17 Khunjompol/Shutterstock.com; p. 18 Kletr/Shutterstock.com; p. 19 naramit/Shutterstock.com; p. 20 Alex Tihonovs/Shutterstock.com; p. 21 Toa55/Shutterstock.com; p. 22 graphego/Shutterstock.com.

Cataloging-in-Publication Data

Names: Sanchez, Micah.
Title: Natural resource depletion / Micah Sanchez.
Description: New York : PowerKids Press, 2018. | Series: Earth's environment in danger | Includes index.
Identifiers: LCCN ISBN 9781538326114 (pbk.) | ISBN 9781538325414 (library bound) | ISBN 9781538326121 (6 pack)
Subjects: LCSH: Natural resources–Juvenile literature. | Conservation of natural resources–Juvenile literature. | Environmental protection–Juvenile literature.
Classification: LCC HC85.S36 2018 | DDC 333.7–dc23

Manufactured in the United States of America

CPSIA Compliance Information: Batch #BW18PK: For Further Information contact Rosen Publishing, New York, New York at 1-800-237-9932

# Contents

# Exhausting What Earth's Given Us

Earth is full of natural resources, which are types of matter found in nature that are valuable to humans. These resources include the air we breathe, the water we drink, and the trees we use to build our houses. However, not all of these natural resources are renewable, or able to be made again by natural processes.

As people continue to use up Earth's natural resources, we're forced to create new ways to produce energy. However, many of these **alternative** energy sources are just a little too late. We're **exhausting** what Earth's given us.

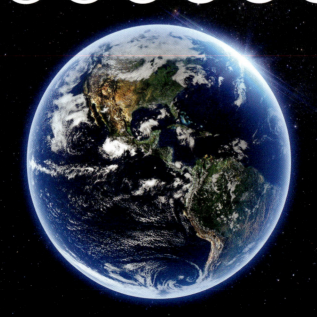

Smog is a type of air pollution that can make it hard to see. **Emissions** from cars, factories, and coal power plants often cause smog.

# Types of Natural Resources

The two types of natural resources are renewable resources and nonrenewable resources. Natural processes can replace renewable resources. Trees are one example of a renewable resource. If you cut down trees, they'll grow again from seeds.

Flow resources are renewable natural resources that don't need to be regrown. Examples of flow resources include wind, the sun, and water. These natural resources are often used as alternative energy sources. They can create wind power, solar power, and hydroelectric power.

Nonrenewable resources will eventually run out or be used up. Some nonrenewable resources are energy sources. These include **fossil fuels**.

## [Danger Alert!]

There are two subtypes of renewable natural resources: **continuous**-flow resources and short-term renewable resources. Wind power is a type of continuous-flow resource. Trees are a type of short-term renewable resource.

Nonrenewable resources are taken from the ground. They can't be grown or replaced and often take millions of years to form. The **minerals** we use to make metals—such as iron used to make steel—are nonrenewable resources.

# Why Are Natural Resources Important?

Natural resources are important for many reasons. The energy we get from natural resources helps power our cars, light and heat our homes, and run our factories.

Natural resources make our lives easier. We can use them to build cars so that we don't have to walk, make clothing so that we can be warm in cold weather, and make medicines so that we don't get sick or can recover.

Today, many natural resources are worth a lot of money. Countries that have raw materials such as wood, iron ore, or crude oil sell them to other countries for economic gain.

wind farm

The crude oil business is very important to Scotland's economy. This oil rig sits in Cromarty Firth near Invergordon, Scotland.

# Causes of Natural Resource Depletion

Humans are responsible for natural resource depletion, which means we've greatly reduced the amount of natural resources. In 1750, the world's population was about 760 million. Today, there are more than 7 billion people living on Earth.

Our ever-growing population has caused a lot of strain on the earth. We have to feed and clothe more people than ever before, build more houses and cars, and deal with new needs for resources.

Because there are so many people living on Earth today, they're using more resources than Earth can produce naturally. Soon, some of these resources will no longer be around!

## [Danger Alert!]

The United States consumes more oil than any other country in the world. The country uses 18.83 million barrels of oil a day. This was about 20.5 percent of the world's daily oil consumption in 2014.

We use coal for many different things. Coal is used to create electricity, produce steel, and make cement.

# The Side Effects

Depleting natural resources can create many issues. If we cut down too many trees at once, many species, or kinds, of plants and animals will lose their homes. New trees can't grow fast enough to replace them in time.

Cutting down trees can also damage the soil. Tree roots help soil absorb, or take in, water. Without trees, some areas might have more flooding. Many forests are cut down to make room for farming. The machinery used to cut down trees is very heavy and causes a large amount of damage to the soil.

## [Danger Alert!]

Trees take in a gas called carbon dioxide during **photosynthesis**. When trees are cut down and burned, they release stored carbon back into the atmosphere. Carbon dioxide is a **greenhouse gas** that adds to **climate change**.

The island of Nauru in the Pacific Ocean has been depleted of a type of salt called phosphate. All that's left are limestone formations. Today, many Nauruans are unhealthy and poor.

# Case Study: Soil Erosion in India

Soil **erosion** in India is a very serious problem. Each year, India loses about 5,880 tons (5,334 mt) of soil due to harmful farming practices such as adding too much **fertilizer** to the soil and spraying crops with too many chemicals to kill bugs and pests.

If the soil in India isn't able to support life, the people of India will suffer. Without healthy soil, healthy crops can't grow and be sold. Scientists have been working hard to find a way to make the soil healthy again so that Indian farmers can continue to grow crops.

## [Danger Alert!]

One of the largest causes of soil erosion is farming. Farmers cut down trees to make room for cropland and space for their animals. In the last 150 years, half the surface soil on the planet has been lost to erosion.

Desertification refers to land becoming desert as a result of human activity. To fight this, organizations such as the World Wildlife Fund, or WWF, work with farmers to use **sustainable** farming practices.

# Conservation Efforts

Conserving, or protecting and preventing the waste of, our natural resources is more important now than ever before. Today, many people around the world have realized that our natural resources might not always be there for us to use.

WWF was started in 1961 as a way to find more financial support for conservation efforts worldwide. In 2016, WWF joined a number of other conservation groups to form the Global Mangrove Alliance. The Global Mangrove Alliance was created to save mangrove **habitats**. Mangrove forests are a bridge between water habitats and land habitats. They are home to many important life-forms.

Mangrove forests help protect coastal areas from storms and other bad weather, provide coastal residents with jobs, and store carbon.

# Alternative Energy Sources

Finding alternative energy sources is a way to help conserve Earth's natural resources. "Green" energy is energy from renewable sources such as wind farms, hydroelectric plants, and solar panels.

biomass
power plant

Biomass, or plant matter and animal waste, can be used to make biofuel. Biofuel made from corn and sugarcane can replace fuels we commonly use today, such as gasoline, diesel, and jet fuel.

While these energy sources still depend on some fossil fuels to work, they greatly reduce the energy industry's use of these fuels. These energy sources don't pollute the environment and can often help people save money on their energy bill. Using alternative energy may lead to people being more mindful of how their other choices affect the earth.

If we continue to use oil as much as we do today, we may run out of oil in the next 40 years or so.

# Helpful Legislation

Today, many people disagree about how to deal with natural resource depletion and conservation. The United Nations works to solve disagreements between countries fighting over natural resources. The UN works toward helping people make use of their land in a sustainable way.

The EPA's first job was to carry out the Clean Air Act of 1970. This act aimed to reduce the amount of air pollution from cars and factories.

In the United States, many different laws and organizations have been created to control the use of natural resources. Certain legislation, or laws, tries to make sure that the government officials consider the environment before they make decisions that will affect it. In 1970, President Richard Nixon created the Environmental Protection Agency to keep an eye on environmental practices.

# What Can You Do?

You can help reduce natural resource depletion by being mindful of how much energy you're using. Turn the lights off when you leave a room. You can also start riding the bus to school instead of having your parents drop you off. If you live close to school, you could walk or ride your bike. Buy a reusable water bottle and fill it up at home so that you don't need to buy bottled water.

Make sure you're separating your garbage and recyclable items. Recycling plastic and other materials such as cardboard and paper can help reduce how much we depend on nonrenewable natural resources.

# Glossary

**alternative:** Different from the usual, offering a choice.

**climate change:** Change in Earth's weather caused by human activity.

**continuous:** Continuing without stopping.

**emission:** Something that is given off.

**erosion:** The wearing away of the earth's surface by wind or water.

**exhaust:** To use up completely.

**fertilizer:** Something added to the soil to help plants grow.

**fossil fuel:** A fuel—such as coal, oil, or natural gas—that is formed in the earth from dead plants or animals.

**greenhouse gas:** Gases in the atmosphere that trap energy from the sun.

**habitat:** The natural home for plants, animals, and other living things.

**mineral:** A naturally occurring solid substance that is not of plant or animal origin.

**photosynthesis:** The way in which green plants make their own food from sunlight, water, and carbon dioxide.

**sustainable:** Able to last a long time.

# Index

# Websites

Due to the changing nature of Internet links, PowerKids Press has developed an online list of websites related to the subject of this book. This site is updated regularly. Please use this link to access the list:
www.powerkidslinks.com/eeid/deplete